The Girl Who Survived

A True Story of the
Holocaust

The Girl Who Survived

A True Story of the
Holocaust

Bronia Brandman
and Carol Bierman

Scholastic Inc.
New York Toronto London Auckland
Sydney Mexico City New Delhi Hong Kong

ISBN 978-0-545-17574-6

12 11 10 9 8 7 6 5 4 3 2 1   10 11 12 13 14 15/0

Printed in the U.S.A.   40
First Scholastic printing, September 2010
Book design by Jennifer Rinaldi Windau

To Bozenka, who risked her life to save mine,
and to Cousin Simon, who brought my brother
and me to the U.S. and took care of me
where Bozenka left off.

— *B.B.*

To Bronia, my brave mentor of the Holocaust
and dear friend.

— *C.B.*

My parents, Tulek, and I were unable to get to

the hiding place in time. We were caught in the roundup.

We were taken to the courtyard of the local school with many

of the other Jews in the town. We understood what this meant.

I knew this was not a good situation, and I saw it reflected

in Tulek's eyes. He looked frightened and worried.

I moved closer to my mother. She looked around

the school yard, then down at me, and softly said, "Run."

I just stared at her, but she said it again. "Run."

It was barely a whisper, but the intensity in her eyes said *Go.*

Go now!

Contents

Introduction

On January 30, 1933, Adolf Hitler, the leader of the National Socialist German Workers' Party (the Nazi Party), was appointed Chancellor of Germany by President Paul von Hindenburg. Following Hindenburg's death on August 2, 1934, Hitler became Germany's absolute dictator, known as *der Führer*, "the Leader." Hitler hated Jews and other groups of people. He had come to power in part by spreading propaganda, insisting that if Germans did not vote for the Nazi Party, the Communists would win, take everyone's possessions, and enslave the people. Many Germans became fearful. Hitler and his followers also let it be known that the Jews were aligned with the Communists and responsible for all of Germany's problems.

In the 1920s and 1930s, the German people had serious problems, such as a high rate of joblessness, which made it difficult to clothe and feed one's family. Hitler focused on a simplistic view of Germany's problems. Instead of seeking solutions, Hitler blamed a scapegoat, the Jews. He told the Germans that the Jews were a pestilence, like lice. He called them monsters and referred to the Jews as less than animals. He hated them for no reason except that they were Jews. This behavior is known as anti-Semitism, an irrational hatred of the Jewish people.

Jews had been loyal German citizens, and many were decorated soldiers who had fought in the German armed forces in World War I. They were good members of the community who contributed to society, taught in the universities, and were proud of their German homeland.

Beginning in 1933, laws were enacted against the Jews, preventing them from doing the simplest things, such as sitting on a park bench or owning a pet dog. Then, in 1935, the Nuremberg Laws were enacted, effectively creating a separation between Jews and non-Jews. Hitler made these laws to make life difficult for the Jews of Germany, and eventually these harsh rules spread throughout much of Europe as the Nazi war machine took over country after country.

The Nuremberg Laws began with just three rules about

racial purity: Jews could not marry non-Jews; Jews and non-Jews could not have children together; and Jews lost their German citizenship, stripping them of political and other rights. Jews were thrown out of their civil service jobs and their numbers were reduced in the professions. Also, students were ousted from colleges and lower schools.

Gradually, the laws restricting Jewish freedoms grew to more than 400. They gained public support because the Nazis continued to spread lies about the Jewish people and made others fearful of them. Many Germans who had been friends and neighbors of the Jews would no longer speak to them. In fact, many Germans turned Jews over to the Nazi authorities for a variety of offenses, such as smuggling food to feed their families and selling things on the black market to survive. The Germans would often be paid a bounty for betraying their Jewish neighbors.

An event called *Kristallnacht* is seen today as the beginning of the end for the Jews of Europe. *Kristallnacht*, which translates as "Night of Broken Glass," began on November 9, 1938, and was a night of terror for the Jews of Germany.

The glass windows of more than 7,500 Jewish shops and department stores were smashed; 267 synagogues (Jewish houses of worship) were desecrated or burned to the ground; and Jews were dragged from their homes, beaten, humiliated, arrested, and killed. Almost 30,000 Jewish men were sent to concentration camps. It marked the beginning of Nazi viciousness on a grand scale.

Eventually, Jews were no longer permitted to live where they wanted and later were not permitted to live at all. After World War II began, when Germany invaded Poland on September 1, 1939, the Nazis began committing mass murder against the Jewish people, killing more than six million Jews, including 1.5 million children. The world stood by as Hitler and his agents wiped out men, women, and children in the hope of ridding the entire world of Jews. The Nazis murdered other people, such as priests, nuns, those who chose to help the Jews, Gypsies, and the disabled.

When Hitler's armies later marched across Europe, they intensified their anti-Jewish persecutions. In most occupied countries, German soldiers and their local followers removed

Jews from their homes and forced them into ghettos, which lacked medical supplies and food. Eventually the Nazis either transported the Jews to concentration or extermination camps, or killed them in their own cities and towns by enlisting the help of the local governments and their police forces.

The Nazis created a network of work camps using mostly Jewish slave labor. These camps were connected with businesses that continued to produce their products or made new ones for the German military. Later, Hitler began the "Final Solution," the mass murder of the Jewish people, by deporting millions of Jews to death camps. The death camp that murdered more Jews than any other, more than one million, was Auschwitz II–Birkenau, located in present-day Poland.

Not everyone in Europe gave in to the Nazis. Some people in German-occupied countries such as Denmark, Albania, and Bulgaria defied the Nazis and saved many Jewish lives. A small number of people in other occupied countries stood up for their Jewish friends, neighbors, and even people they did not know. Despite great personal risk, they hid Jews, fed them, gave them safe havens, or engineered their escape.

Sometimes these good people were caught helping Jews and were punished with death. Today those brave protectors are called the "Righteous Among the Nations." They have been honored in Israel with their name engraved on the walls of the Garden of the Righteous and a tree planted in their name in the garden on the Mount of Remembrance in Jerusalem.

By 1944, the tide of the war began to turn against Germany. Beginning in July, the advancing Soviet Red Army began liberating some concentration camps on the Eastern Front. In April 1945, American forces began liberating camps on the Western Front. As the Allies began converging on Berlin, Germany's capital, in the hopes of capturing and defeating Hitler, they discovered that he had committed suicide in his underground bunker on April 30. On May 8, 1945, the war in Europe ended. Unfortunately, it was too late to save the lives of millions of innocent people. But Hitler's Final Solution was ended.

Bronia Rubin Brandman was only eight years old when the German Army invaded her country of Poland. This is her unforgettable story of courage and survival.

CHAPTER 1
My Grandfather's House

I was lucky to be born in the house that my grandfather Eliasz Mandelbaum built. It was a big house, and it needed to be, because he had twelve children. The Mandelbaum home was L-shaped and covered two blocks in our town of Jaworzno, Poland. By the time I was born there in 1931 — and like many babies at the time, I was actually born in the house — my grandfather was an old man. He died in 1933, and I never really got to know him. But family members have shared many stories about him. He was a prosperous businessman, well-known in Poland, who manufactured and sold liqueurs and wine. He also produced these products in the neighboring country of Hungary, where he owned orchards of various fruits such as plums and peaches, from which he made the fruit brandies called slivowitz.

Grandfather often traveled to find good land for more vineyards to expand his business. He ran the business from

1

top to bottom, starting with the growing of the fruit and ending with the sale of the finished product. On one such trip with one of my uncles, Grandfather had a large amount of cash with him, I guess to pay for the land he wanted to purchase. When he removed the money from his pocket, a great wind blew the money everywhere. As people came out of their homes to grab the flying money, Grandfather did not chase after the bills. He simply said, "Good. Now many people who could not otherwise afford it will have dowries for their daughters' marriages." He was a wise and generous man who cared about people.

In the backyard of our home, a large area that my family called "the Burgh," my grandfather had several warehouses, where he manufactured and stored his products. There were several other buildings out in the back, including a synagogue and a caretaker's house. The rest was open space, great for playing games. Kids from all over town came to our backyard to play, and at any time they could find games in progress.

The boys' favorite game was soccer, and we also played dodgeball, tag, hide-and-seek, and jump rope. In the winter, we went ice-skating and sledding on nearby streets, which were icy and steep. We would slide so fast down those streets that we'd end up all the way in the market square, which was in front of our house. My little sister Rutka was a brave kid in my eyes. She would zoom down the steep street, laughing all the way.

On the street level of our house were several stores. These stores belonged to my aunts and uncles, my grandfather's children. There was Aunt Surele, who owned a tile store; Aunt Esther Malka had a fabric store; my parents had a hardware store; and Uncle Wolf and Uncle Shulem had a liquor store.

I was waiting for my aunt Esther Malka to get some special material in her store, because my mother had promised that she would have a party dress made especially for me. I decided that it had to be orange organza, an elegant and fairylike material. I never did get that dress, because life soon changed and party dresses were the furthest thing from our minds.

There were other stores, but the children's favorite was the ice cream store. My cousins and I often spent our allowance there. My favorite ice cream flavor was vanilla, but the store sold other treats, too. I usually alternated between buying ice cream and a luscious strawberry jam–filled doughnut. Yum! One of my other favorite snacks was crunchy pickles.

Upstairs, above the stores, were the actual living quarters. During the time my grandfather lived in the house, it had many bedrooms. There was a salon, which is a huge fancy living room. Because my grandfather often invited the poor strangers who came through town to dine with the family on Shabbat (the sabbath day), there could be as many as forty people in the room at one time. It also had a dining room, kitchen, and even a separate apartment, just for Passover.

Passover is one of my favorite holidays. It lasts for eight days. On this holiday, the whole family would congregate at my grandfather's home, dressed in their best clothes, and have two Seders together, on two consecutive nights. A Seder is a festive meal where we retell the story of how the Jews escaped from slavery in Egypt.

The Seders were held in the special apartment. On Passover, Jews traditionally do not eat bread or bread products. We only eat matzoh, which is made from flour and water, baked in only eighteen minutes, and never permitted to rise. The apartment was kept empty all year except for the week of Passover, so that no one had to worry there might be even one leftover crumb of any type of bread there.

Ours was a big house, yet it was missing a few essential rooms that one might expect in a home today. For example, there were no interior bathrooms! There was an outhouse in the backyard. It was cold out there in the winter, especially if you had to go in the middle of the night! And because the outhouse was not connected to a sewer system, it didn't smell so good, either. There were two other toilets in stalls. One was on the balcony to my family's apartment, and the other was on my aunt's balcony next to ours. This was a little better, because at least you didn't have to go downstairs to go to the bathroom and you did get some privacy. But it was still cold and smelly!

The apartments were connected with doors from one apartment to another, so that one didn't have to go outside to visit with anyone else. When my grandfather was alive, our house had beautiful furnishings. I still remember the beautiful red velvet sofa in the parlor.

In addition to religious holidays and Bar Mitzvahs, the birth of children was another cause for celebration. Every new child was named in the synagogue before the entire community. Girls were named at the first service the community had after her birth. Boys were named on the eighth day after their birth.

Engagements and weddings were other events that brought the whole community together. Everyone partook of these happy events and came to wish *Mazel tov*, good luck, to the parents and the happy couple. Oddly enough, our family did not celebrate birthdays and anniversaries. One reason was that the local population did not celebrate those events unless the family was quite wealthy.

In those days, parents did not tell children where babies came from. Instead, kids were told that a stork flew over the house and dropped the new baby from the air. I had seen storks sitting on the roofs of houses. So I often went up into my aunt's attic and waited and waited. Unfortunately for me, the storks never arrived, but miraculously, new babies in our family did.

In front of our stores was a sidewalk where we girls could play hopscotch. About every two weeks, the local farmers brought their produce to our town for sale, and they would set up stalls in the marketplace, which was in the open space in front of the stores. The farmers and their families displayed every type of vegetable and fruit that grew in the region, such as potatoes, tomatoes, onions, cucumbers, cabbage, and cauliflower.

Market day was an exciting event for kids. We would run from wagon to wagon and stall to stall to see what was for sale. In addition to selling food, vendors might offer furniture, bedding, and handmade velvet quilts. Some even brought goats, sheep, cows, and horses to sell.

CHAPTER 2
My Family

I was raised in a big family, as was the custom. There were six children in my family. Some of my cousins' families were even bigger.

I was the fourth-born in my family. Mila, born in 1923, was the oldest. She was beautiful and charming, and I loved her dearly. However, she did not always feel that way about me. In fact, I was told she was jealous of me when I was born. Because she had been the only girl in our family until my birth, she was the "princess" and enjoyed her status. When I came along, she let her feelings be known. She was discovered one day brushing my hair with a shoe brush. She explained that she was just making the baby beautiful!

Mila loved fashionable clothes, and my mother had them made-to-order for her because there were no malls or stores that had ready-made clothes off the rack. Mila wore tall boots to the knee and her clothes were copied from Parisian styles.

She wore wide belts, which showed off her beautifully thin waistline.

She had lots of friends and everyone loved her, but not as much as I did. Of all my siblings, I was most enamored with Mila. In fact, I adored her. If Mila went to the movies, I followed her like a puppy. If she went to meet her friends, many of whom were our cousins, I tagged along. Even though she was eight years older than me, I wanted to be with her and her friends. I was a real pest!

I remember a wonderful vacation that I went on with Mila and many cousins around her age. The young people were offered the option of choosing between going to a summer camp or renting a cottage in the woods under the supervision of a young aunt. They chose the cottage. Because my goal was to be around Mila all the time, I begged and begged to be allowed to go on this vacation. They were going to the village of Alwernia, southeast of Jaworzno. It was a beautiful country area. Vacationers could swim in a river, make campfires at night, and sing songs. But there were also some chores involved. The cottage had no running water, so the kids took turns carrying water from the well. They placed a pole across their shoulders and hung a bucket of water from each end. It was heavy, but even Mila took a turn!

I wanted to go so badly on that vacation that I pestered Mila until she finally gave in and took me along. I really was a pest! There wasn't even a bed for me, so I had to sleep curled up in a crib. I didn't care that when I woke up in the morning I was stiff from sleeping in a weird position, and it took a while for me to stand straight. I would have done anything to be with Mila and her friends. It was wonderful, the best vacation ever!

Mendek was next in the family. He was born in 1926 and was very creative. He was not so interested in school. He liked math and often thought of it as a game, because it came easily to him. He helped my father in the hardware store. They both invented things. Mendek was quiet; he never made a fuss about anything. I thought he was a little strange because he never complained. All the other kids complained, including me! He even mended his own socks, which was unusual for a boy, because sewing was considered women's work.

He was usually one of the first up in the house, especially during the war, because he had to leave early to work in the coal mines. He had to rise so early that the stove was not yet lit. There wasn't much food at that time, but he never said a word, he just ate raw radishes and did what he had to do. Later, in 1941, when the Nazis came to find Mila and send her to a forced-labor camp, Mendek volunteered to go in her place.

We were not sure where they would send him, nor what he would find when he got there. And yet he volunteered to save his sister from this harsh unknown. Nothing would change his mind. I could not believe how brave and selfless he was.

Mendek was moved from camp to camp. He was in nine camps throughout the war, both forced-labor camps and concentration camps. At one time he was in Flossenbürg, a concentration camp in the Oberpfalz region of Bavaria, Germany, near the prewar border with Czechoslovakia. The camp was established in March 1938 and liberated in April 1945. During that time more than 96,000 prisoners passed through Flossenbürg, and approximately 30,000 died there.

As Mendek spent time in each camp, he learned the tricks of survival. For example, he was given a slice of bread every evening. That was the ration for the whole day. Mendek was a disciplined person. He ate only half the slice and saved the other half for breakfast. This was both a good and bad idea. It was good because that little bit of breakfast kept him going through the day. It was a bad idea because if other starving inmates learned that you had food in your pocket, they could beat you or even kill you for it.

My next oldest brother, Tulek, was born in 1928 and was the opposite of Mendek. Tulek was a mischief maker. He "marched to his own drummer." School and learning were not his strong points, nor of much interest to him. I am sure this was disappointing to my father, who came from a long line of scholars, all of whom excelled at studying. I know that my father would have loved it and been quite proud if his sons were good students. However, Tulek had other interests. He always had a twinkle in his eye, and even my father did not scare him. He just went about his business without anyone's permission. He always came home after everyone was asleep.

That way he did not have to explain to anyone where he had been or what he had been up to.

You might think that because he missed dinner with the family, Tulek might go hungry. Not resourceful Tulek! Eating a good meal was never a problem. At any time he could find a meal at one of our aunts' apartments. They were always glad to see him and provide the needed food. The cousins, aunts, and uncles loved him because he could fix anything, such as toys, bikes, and locks, and he also taught the kids how to ride bikes.

Tulek and I did not get along so well. He took my allowance and beat me up on a regular basis. I did not understand why he did this, because I got along well with everyone else. Sometimes, when Tulek beat me up to steal my allowance, Mendek came to my rescue. He would beat up Tulek in return for beating me up, and he even rescued my allowance for me. Mendek was truly a caring brother.

Even so, I secretly admired Tulek. He got away with almost everything, although Father was not about to excuse some of the things Tulek got into. So he often punished Tulek with a spanking. In those days, children were not punished by losing privileges. After all, there was no television or computer to take away. For the most part, Tulek was a happy-go-lucky, carefree kid. If only I could have been like that!

I was the next-born in the family. I must admit that I was a little roly-poly. I really liked food. I ate at every one of my aunts' houses. I would go to the first aunt and have a big hamburger. Then I would visit another aunt's apartment and have a smaller hamburger and a little rhubarb for dessert. This dessert was mixed with strawberries and lots of sugar. It was wonderful and I loved it. My cousins often stopped me in the street and asked what I had eaten that day. I would list every morsel.

But when I realized that the other kids were making fun of me for my love of food, I was embarrassed and stopped eating. I grew thinner. My mother became alarmed about my health. In those days, a chubby child was considered healthy. My mother offered to pay me the equivalent of a nickel if I would eat what she put on my plate. That was a lot of money for a kid, just to eat! Unfortunately for my mother, I did not take her up on her offer, and I continued to get thinner until I lost all of my "baby fat." Eventually I began eating about the same as everyone else in my family.

When I was about three years old, my first and favorite book was *Chicken Little*, written in Polish. Someone would read it to me. As I got older, I looked forward to going to school, so I could learn to read by myself. I wanted to be like the bigger kids in my extended family. Frankly, I considered kids my own age to be boring.

Finally, when I was seven years old, I did get to attend school for a while, but the teacher didn't like the Jewish students. During recess, we went outside without the teacher, and the other children took advantage of her absence. We were afraid they would beat us up because they had been taught to hate the Jews, so sometimes we went across the street from the school and stood near a bakery for safety. They would not beat us up if there were adults around. School turned out to be not that much fun.

The Germans invaded Poland on September 1, 1939, in a blitzkrieg. Blitzkrieg means "lightning war," in which planes, tanks, and fast-moving troops are used to take over a country. When the Germans attacked Poland, they attacked ruthlessly and bombed Polish cities, reducing many to rubble.

Even towns and cities that escaped bombing were subjected to harsh measures against the Jews. Many prohibitions took effect immediately after occupation, and by the end of 1939, the public schools no longer allowed Jewish children to attend.

Not only were we Jewish children not allowed to attend school with the others. We could not go to parks. We were forbidden to meet in groups or even just to pray. Our mail was censored, and newspapers were forbidden to us. Many neighborhoods were restricted. If Jews were found walking there, they could be arrested.

We were not allowed to own radios, bicycles, or pets, all of which the authorities confiscated. We had to turn in all fur coats, which were sent to German soldiers on the Eastern Front, and all objects made of gold, silver, and copper, including jewelry and religious objects. Possessing any of these items or breaking any of the rules would bring swift and severe punishment.

So we did what Jews had done for centuries whenever they were forbidden to learn. We created secret schools, including one in Jaworzno. The Bais Yaakov School taught Jewish subjects such as the Hebrew language, Jewish history, prayer, and the holy texts. It was dangerous for students to attend this forbidden school, and it was dangerous for the teachers to teach there. Despite the risks, students attended classes and teachers taught as long as they could. Eventually the schools closed, because they were so dangerous to attend.

That was the end of my formal education for the next seven years. Before the war, my parents had arranged for an itinerant tutor. It was hard for Jewish teachers to get jobs in schools even though they were qualified, so they often traveled from place to place looking for work to teach privately in people's homes. My father also tutored us. He even taught his children to speak German, because it was considered the language of culture. I hung around as he tried to teach Tulek. Just by listening to them, I learned to speak German.

I was considered to be a stubborn child by my family. Actually, I thought I was rather lazy. I liked to sleep late, so I was never around to do the morning chores. It was inexpensive to hire people to work in one's home, and most people who were middle-class had a maid. One morning when our maid thought I was still asleep, I heard her tell her visiting friend how wonderful Rutka was. Then she pointed at me and said, "This one is good for nothing."

Hearing that had a profound impact on my behavior. I did not want to be thought of in that way. So when the war started and we no longer had a maid, we children had to do many of the chores. Because school was closed, I could have been playing, but to counteract what the maid had said about me, I began to work around the house. I scrubbed the wooden floors. I peeled potatoes. I even took it one step further by helping my aunts clean their apartments. This work was difficult for me, and I wasn't good at any of it, but I tried hard to change their perception of me.

In some ways it was lucky that I tried to do all of these things. I learned to survive later in the ghetto and camps because of my new attitude. I had learned to adapt to a variety of situations. I had learned to endure difficulties, hard work, and most important of all, I became alert to my surroundings. This probably saved my life many times.

After me, Rutka was born in 1933. She was my opposite. She always did what was expected of her and more. She got up with the roosters at the crack of dawn. She finished all her chores before I even got out of bed. In fact, she often did my chores. And she shared a bed with me! She was a sweet child, playful and fun to be around.

Hana Macia, born in 1937, was the baby. We called her Macia. I discovered that Father thought she was the most beautiful and smartest of his children. I was a little surprised to learn this. I actually thought she was just average! However, many years later, when I came to the United States, my cousin Simon told me that every time a new baby was born in my family, my father would write to him, saying that he believed that this new baby was the cutest and the smartest! He was tender and solicitous with Macia.

I want to tell you about both of my parents. My father, Israel, was handsome, with a dark, closely cropped beard. He was a genius. Everyone knew how smart he was. He studied all of our holy books, and he built things just by duplicating the original object. He built and connected a phone from our house to our hardware store. He wasn't much of a businessman, so running the store was not his first love. He much preferred doing things he was better at, such as making toys for us. I remember that he built a hobby horse for Macia. He also built a dollhouse with furniture for all the girls to share.

But my father had a stern side, too. You did not joke with him, and he rarely smiled. He did not engage in chitchat with the children and never praised our work to our faces. One time I saw him showing my homework from the public school to my uncle and telling him what a good job I had done. Up until then, I hadn't realized that Father even knew I did any homework! When he turned around and saw me standing there, he became red in the face. He did not want us to know that he was proud of each of us.

Mother, on the other hand, was sweet, gentle, and beautiful. She dressed fashionably and wore beautiful hats. Her Yiddish name was Ittel, but she was known as Eda. She and my father were married on September 13, 1921. She lovingly cared for her husband and children and protected them, as most mothers do. She shopped and cooked for her family, did the cleaning with the help of the maid, and oversaw the laundry. She often helped my father in the hardware store. She was a cheerful and pleasant person who did not yell. She loved to dance. Sometimes we even had a dance teacher for the girls, and to this day I still love to dance. It was fun!

Our life as a family went smoothly until I was eight years old. We were like most other families except that we were surrounded by my mother's eleven brothers and sisters, their husbands, wives, and children, which gave us built-in friends and protectors. We got along well with our neighbors, we shopped at their stores, and for the most part everyone respected one another. Life was fun, quiet, and, most of all, "normal."

CHAPTER 3
Life Changes

After the Germans launched their invasion of Poland in 1939, Hitler's laws against Jews began to affect our lives. In some occupied towns, the Nazis started rounding up Jews. The roundups were always a surprise and often took place on the Sabbath or important Jewish holidays. Sometimes the authorities let the Jews return to their homes, but sometimes they removed people from their families and sent them to slave-labor camps or to forced labor in the coal mines.

Just before the invasion, my parents noticed that the situation in Jaworzno was changing rapidly, and not for the better. They decided it might be safer if we visited with one of my uncles who lived in Mielec, a small town northeast of Krakow. Father and Mendek remained behind to look after the store. Mother took the rest of the children on the train. It was crowded. Lots of Jews were moving inland in Poland, away from the German border.

We had to get off the train in Krakow, because only Polish soldiers could continue to ride eastward from there. No civilians were permitted on the trains. So Mother rented an open wagon with a driver, and we rode all night. It was a freezing-cold, bumpy, and scary ride, but thankfully we arrived safely.

Back in Jaworzno, things were not good. The Nazis came to Father's store and forced him and Mendek down into the basement, where they made them face the wall. They ordered Father to stand with his hands in the air. They pointed guns at his back and threatened to shoot him. They made him stand that way for a long time, laughing and making fun of him, then let him go.

Father was so upset by the Nazis' treatment that he could not bear to return to our store. He was traumatized by this incident. Father and Mendek then went to a nearby town, where they stayed in the home of a family that had run away to Krakow.

Many Jewish families fled their homes in an effort to find safety. As they entered another town, they would approach the homes of people they knew or who someone had mentioned might offer them a safe haven. Often the residents had fled, but had left their homes open for whoever needed them for safety. Jews knew that where family was concerned, they would not be turned away, and that all Jews were considered family.

Shortly after our arrival in Mielec, the war began. Soon the Nazis systematically went from house to house, banging on doors. They banged on the door of my uncle's house. *"Juden, raus, raus, schnell, schnell!"* they screamed at us — "Jews, out, out, fast, fast!" They ordered us out with rifles pointed at us. Slowly the family went into the street wearing only their pajamas and nightgowns. Many neighbors were experiencing the same situation.

The Nazis gathered many of the Jewish men in the town and took them to the synagogue. It was Rosh Hashanah, September 14, 1939. They locked them in and poured gasoline all around the outside of the building. Then the Germans lit the gasoline, and the building began to burn. We were horrified. The Nazis made sure no one could get away.

Some of the men tried to escape through the windows, but the Nazis shot them. Everyone in that building was murdered. It was so scary and sad.

My mother decided to return to Jaworzno with her children. However, Poland was still at war, and it took four weeks until the war was over and our country was defeated. It was not until sometime later that we could return to Jaworzno.

By September 29, 1939, the Germans occupied the western half of our country. The other half of Poland was given to the Soviet Union. Prior to the war, the Soviets had made a secret treaty with the Nazis, which stated that if Germany conquered Poland, the Soviet Union and Germany each would receive half of Poland. In return, neither Germany nor the Soviet Union would oppose the other.

The Poles tried to defend against the German invasion, but their army was no match for the Nazi war machine. The German Army had state-of-the-art planes, tanks, and guns, and was much more powerful than the Polish armed forces.

After occupying their half of Poland, the Nazis began a reign of terror. They began to round up Jews and deport them to concentration and slave-labor camps. No one knew what to expect in these camps. It was in one of those roundups that the Germans came to take Mila to a labor camp and Mendek volunteered to go in her place. This was so brave, because we had no idea where he would be going or what hardships he would have to endure. I was sad and scared, because I did not think I would ever see Mendek again. There were many more roundups in Jaworzno. I remember one in particular. It happened during the day, and the soldiers again yelled, "Jews out!" They entered our homes, made us form a single line, and marched us to the market square. Just seeing their Nazi uniforms was terrifying. And they had guns pointed at us.

As the German soldier inside our home ordered us out, I took a risk. Because I was small and was standing behind the soldier, I slipped behind the front door and hid. When he exited and closed the door, I remained in the house. I was all alone and did not know if I would ever see my family again. Remember, I was stubborn! I was not going to let the Nazis tell me what to do.

Later in the day, to my surprise and joy, my family returned home. My mother was happy to see me, because she did not know what had happened to me. She was even happier that I was not with them, because one could never predict if the Germans would let us return to our homes or send us to camps. As it was, we were all safe for now, and I guess being stubborn worked out for the better that time.

CHAPTER 4
I Become a Smuggler

Jews were forbidden to live and walk where they pleased. They were not allowed on restricted streets. The Gestapo, the Nazi secret police, gave orders to confiscate some Jewish homes, which were seized with everything still inside. Evicted owners could not take even personal items. These homes were used to house German officers and the offices of the Gestapo. No accommodations were made for these Jews when their homes were seized. They depended on the kindness of other family members or Jewish friends.

We were lucky to be able to remain in our own home. Because there was some extra room in the large parlor, we were able to take in a cousin, his wife, his sister, and her husband. Four extra people easily fit in the spare space. We were used to having extended family nearby.

The most difficult thing to obtain was food, which was scarce and rationed. By this time I was nine years old. It was 1940, and I volunteered to be the family smuggler. My parents agreed that I would be the best choice to leave our neighborhood and visit the stores of the Gentiles (non-Jews) to trade things we had hidden just after the Germans arrived. My family could now exchange these items on the black market for things we needed. The black market was not a real store, but an exchange between two people. Just about anything could be sold on the black market.

My family thought it was a good idea for me to be the smuggler because I was small and had self-confidence. I also did not look particularly Jewish. I had a petite nose, and my hair was dirty blonde. Not looking obviously Jewish was an advantage, because it made me inconspicuous and less likely to be stopped by German soldiers on the street.

My family believed that I could pass for a Polish peasant girl. They also thought that I was not afraid of anything. I would cover myself with a large shawl so that no one could see my big yellow Jewish star. All Jews were required to wear a Star of David sewn on the front and back of their clothing near the shoulder. The star had the word *Jude* printed on it, which means "Jew" in German. This made it easy to identify who was Jewish. Little did anyone know that under that peasant shawl beat the heart of a scared Jewish girl.

Also under the shawl, I would hide a bolt of material that I was going to trade that day. I would march right past the soldiers and out of our restricted area. The soldiers must have believed that I was a Christian peasant girl, because none ever bothered me. My aunt had some bolts of material from her store that she had been able to hide. I would take one of those bolts and head out for a store owned by Gentiles. Although this store sold food, material to make clothing was prized because it was difficult to get, so the store owners were willing to trade.

I deliberately walked the long way to get to the store so that no one would suspect what I was up to. I avoided farms, because they almost always had dogs. Dogs would bark and alert the farmers that an intruder was nearby. Anyone noticing me could lead to disaster.

I entered the rear of the store and waited until I could get an owner's attention. Then I would bargain privately with the owner. The owners trusted me and would not bargain with anyone else in my family, because they knew I took many precautions getting to and from their store, which protected them from detection. It was important that no one knew the store owners were trading with Jews. This was a severely punishable offense, and no one wanted to get caught. Bargaining was the easy part. Getting to the store and passing any German soldiers were the hard parts. Every time I walked in front of those soldiers, I was sure they were going to shoot me for being a smuggler.

In various places in Poland, young boys would sneak out of the ghettos through spaces in the walls. Ghettos were restricted and confined areas where Nazis forced Jews to relocate. Some ghettos were surrounded by walls and barbed wire. The boys who snuck out were so thin from malnutrition that they could squeeze through narrow openings. They would smuggle back potatoes hidden in their pants. They took the potatoes from nearby farms or storage areas that belonged to the Poles. Their pant legs, tight at the bottom, would bulge with their prizes. Smuggling kept many families alive. But if you were caught, it was punishable by death. Many child smugglers were killed just for trying to bring food to their families.

I might trade the material for butter, flour, eggs, or even sugar, which was scarce in Poland. Sometimes I was lucky and was able to trade for larger amounts of food. The items I smuggled back home were never used by my family. They were resold on the black market; then someone else in the family bought potatoes. We could buy enough potatoes to feed the whole family with the money obtained from just a single pound of butter. We made everything from those potatoes. My mother was very creative and figured out how to imitate gefilte fish, a traditional Jewish food, with potatoes. She even devised a cake from potatoes!

Smuggling was a risky and scary business for a nine-year-old girl. Each time I went out, my mother worried. She never knew if I would return. I could see the pain and fear in her eyes whenever I went on one of my trips.

One time there was a great deal of snow on the ground. I insisted on wearing Mila's boots, only because they belonged to Mila. Because I was the smuggler, my mother could not say no to me. I could do whatever I wanted and get away with it. My mother could not convince me that it was a bad idea to wear the boots because they had big holes. I wore them anyway! I trudged through snow up to my knees. The snow got in and soaked through my three pairs of socks, making them heavy and wet. This made walking difficult, but I had to wear those boots!

A few days later I was sick. One thing we never had was medicine or doctors to help us through an illness. We just had to wait and pray. Luckily, I got better, but smuggling became harder, and we were running out of textiles to trade. Although less smuggling meant less food, my mother and I were happy when my smuggling activities finally stopped.

CHAPTER 5
My Parents Are Taken

In late August 1942, there was another roundup. This time we thought our family was prepared. We all had hiding places outside our home. It was just a question of getting to our safe places before the Nazis reached us. Mila managed to get away with my two baby sisters to a hiding place. On the roof of part of our house there was a sukkah, a temporary structure with four walls and no permanent roof used to celebrate the Jewish holiday of Sukkot.

My family had pre-loosened the baseboards just below the seat of the wooden bench that was in the sukkah. Beneath this bench was a hollow area that contained a window to the attic of this part of the house at one end. Mila and my sisters crawled in beneath the bench, pulled the wooden panels back into place, and went through the window to the attic of the adjoining building. No one could see them or know where they went. It was a good hiding place.

However, my parents, Tulek, and I were unable to get there in time. We were caught in the roundup. We were taken to the courtyard of the local school with many of the other Jews in the town. We understood what this meant. I knew this was not a good situation, and I saw it reflected in Tulek's eyes. He looked frightened and worried.

I moved closer to my mother. She looked around the school yard, then down at me, and softly said, "Run." I just stared at her, but she said it again. "Run." It was barely a whisper, but the intensity in her eyes said, *Go. Go now!*

I know this must have been hard for her to do. She knew that we were not going to be released this time, because in the past we had been released in two to three hours. This time many hours had already passed. Our fate seemed sealed. She knew she would never see me again if I ran, or that the soldiers might shoot me right there in front of her if I attempted to flee. But she wanted me to take the chance. The chance to live!

I slipped away and fortunately was not noticed. I wanted to go to my sisters' hiding place. But I knew that if someone followed me, they would all be caught, too. Instead, I realized that I was not far from a farm where the farmer knew our family. Before the war, each day one of the children in our family would accompany our maid with a pail to the farmer's barn. He would milk the cow as we watched, and we would pay for it. He knew each member of my family.

I went to the neighbor's farm without arousing suspicion or having anyone notice me. I entered the couple's house and asked if I could stay until nightfall. They agreed to let me stay. We were all taking a big chance. They could have turned me in, because it was common to get paid for turning Jews in to the Gestapo. Or we all might get arrested and shot, because it was a crime to shelter Jews. The Gestapo often questioned local farmers and searched their homes and barns to see if they were hiding any Jews. The Gestapo was ruthless and often tortured people to obtain information about Jews.

They were an old couple who had no children of their own. The old man was blind, and I began to think that maybe I could stay with them until the war was over. It seemed like a good place to hide in plain sight. I knew they could use my help around the farm, and I would have a safe place from the

Nazis, as well as food to eat.

I didn't think anyone would question it if the couple suddenly had a niece staying with them, because many people moved around during the war. Children especially went to stay with relatives who lived away from the big cities. The cities could experience severe food shortages, while the countryside had farms that grew food. The countryside was a safer place for children.

But as I thought it through, I realized that by staying with the old couple, I would have to give up being Jewish. No eating kosher, no keeping the Sabbath, none of the Jewish holidays. This made me sad. I was proud of my Jewish heritage. I struggled with the conflict between a safe haven versus continuing my way of life.

I could not give up what I had been taught my whole life; I desperately wanted to remain Jewish. I could have talked it over with the old couple. After all, they were sitting right in front of me. Instead, when it grew dark outside, I quietly walked away from the farm and found my three sisters in our hiding place. Of course I was careful not to let anyone follow me.

CHAPTER 6
To the Ghetto

We girls knew that our parents and Tulek were gone forever. They were loaded onto trucks and taken away. They were sent to Auschwitz, where they were murdered. We realized that we were no longer safe in our town, which had been cleared of Jews. My three sisters and I ran under the cover of darkness to the next town, Sosnowiec. We were unable to take anything with us. No changes of clothing or food.

We were devastated over the deaths of our parents and brother, so we did not think of our own comfort. We did not dare return to our home to get any of our things for fear of being arrested. We were wearing summer clothes, and it was starting to get cooler, especially at night. Only Mila had a beautiful hand-knitted sweater that she must have grabbed before she went into hiding with our two little sisters.

We ran away from Jaworzno to Sosnowiec. It took two nights to get there because we had to walk and could only move at night. We could not use major roads because we did not want to get caught by the Nazis or the Poles. When we finally arrived, we desperately needed a place to live.

For the first few days we stayed in an outdoor lumber yard. I soon found out the good news that there was a law in Sosnowiec that entitled children under twelve a place to stay in the town, and we would be given food-ration cards. Unfortunately, this meant that Mila, who was nineteen, would have to stay in hiding most of the time. If she were seen on the street, she could be arrested. Rutka, Macia, and I would share our rations with Mila. We found a small house that had several rooms. We were assigned to one room for the four of us.

We were always quite hungry. Sometimes the younger girls looked as if they were going to cry, but they did not. During this terrible time, even the youngest children understood that crying did not get them anything. No one could make food, clothing, or blankets magically appear. So children didn't ask and didn't cry.

One day, Mila told me to stay with my sisters and look

after them. She was going out and would be back soon. This was dangerous, because she had no papers allowing her to be in the town. If she was caught, she would be sent to a concentration camp or shot.

It seemed like she was gone a long time. After finally returning home, she had a luminous smile. That was unusual. I asked where she had been and why she was smiling. From her pockets she took out two beautiful pears. We had not seen fruit in such a long time. I looked at Mila and was about to ask how she accomplished this feat, when I noticed that the gold heart-shaped locket that Mila always wore around her neck was missing.

Mila had taken a terrible chance in keeping the beautiful locket. Jews had to turn in all of their possessions, especially jewelry, to the Nazis some time ago. She had not given up the locket, because to Mila it was precious. Mila had kept it hidden under the neckline of her dress. No one had ever noticed it, which was lucky, because a person could be shot for keeping something like this from the Nazis.

I said, "Oh, Mila, you used your necklace to buy the pears."

I was sad for her, but she just kept her glorious smile as we sat around the table and cut the first pear into equal fourths. Then we cut the second pear in half, cutting one half into four equal pieces. We put the other half away for the next day and went to sleep. It was the best pear I ever ate.

In October, the whole Jewish population of the area was forced to move to the ghetto. We were assigned to a small house that had only one room. Eventually two of my aunts and their families also came to Sosnowiec. They were considered illegal in the town, so they could live with us only in secret. Our one-room house was suddenly populated by thirteen people, because we took them in, of course! This reunion was bittersweet because all of us had experienced the loss of loved ones.

The house was primitive. It had a table, chairs, a few mattresses on the floor that we all shared, and no closets or curtains. No one had much food, and the ration cards we were given did not go far to feed even the four of us sisters. Once again my smuggling skills were needed.

My aunts had some money with them. So this time I would

be smuggling live chickens into the ghetto. I would sneak out of the ghetto, purchase a chicken from a nearby farmer, and put the chicken under my arm beneath the shawl with just the right amount of pressure to hold it in place. If I held it too tight, the chicken might squawk. If it was too loose, the chicken could get away. Either scenario would not be good for me.

If I was not careful in front of the guards, I could be shot for smuggling. My family never ate the chicken. Instead we sold it for enough money to buy potatoes and some bread to keep my family going for barely a week.

During the time we lived in Sosnowiec, we were still able to send and receive mail. We tried to keep in contact with Mendek. Through one of his letters, we knew that he was in a forced-labor camp where the workers were making a green powder. Mendek wrote that about a thousand workers had died from handling that green powder. He also wrote that the *kapo*, one of the Jewish inmates who was appointed to maintain order in the barracks, had parents in the Sosnowiec ghetto.

Mila hunted through the ghetto and found where the *kapo*'s family lived. She went to see his parents and brought the beautiful sweater that she had taken by chance from our home before going into hiding. She gave the sweater to them as a gift. She told them of Mendek's situation, and they wrote to their son, to try to help Mendek, and he assigned Mendek to stoke the camp's cooking ovens, which kept him away from the deadly green powder. That sweater had saved his life.

CHAPTER 7
Auschwitz

We were not safe in Sosnowiec for long. In August 1943, the Germans rounded us up from the ghetto to make Sosnowiec *Judenrein*—"cleansed of Jews." The Germans sent us in a train to the Auschwitz concentration camp.

Auschwitz was thirty-seven miles west of Krakow, just south of our hometown, Jaworzno, near the prewar German-Polish border. Auschwitz was the largest concentration camp created by the Nazis. It was really a complex of camps, including the concentration camp, where people were forced to live in barracks and usually died of starvation, disease, beatings, and/or useless labor that wore them out; an extermination camp named Auschwitz II–Birkenau, where they systematically murdered thousands of people a day; and Auschwitz III–Buna-Monowitz, a forced-labor camp. Thirty-four corporations operated in Buna, such as IBM, Siemens, IG Farben, and its many subsidiaries such as Bayer. Using slave labor, these companies created materials for the German war effort, such as synthetic rubber, plastics, and plane parts.

The train ride was awful and scary. We were jammed into a cattle car with about one hundred other people. Before the war, when cattle were transported in those cars, care was taken to limit the number of cows in each car so as not to damage the cattle. When the Germans put Jews in those same cars, they packed us in so tightly that we could not sit down. The car we were in smelled badly and people were getting sick, making the situation even worse.

The conditions on these trains were horrible. In summer, it was stiflingly hot. In winter, it was freezing and icicles hung from the sides of the car. The boards that made up the sides of the car had small cracks between them, allowing the wind to whistle through.

There were no windows in those cars. There was no bathroom; a bucket was the only accommodation. Privacy was nonexistent. People tried hard to be kind and not stare whenever someone used the bucket. There was no food or water throughout the trip.

Trips could take many days, and some people died from heat or cold, thirst, and hunger. In the heat of summer, many died of thirst. The winter, at least, afforded people a small drink by melting the icicles that hung from the cars.

Our train ride was relatively short, because Sosnowiec was near Auschwitz. Thankfully, we did not experience some of those terrible conditions on the trains. However, it was August and hot. There was silence in my car. No one on the train exchanged a word. We had already heard about Auschwitz and what took place there, so we knew that these probably were our last hours on Earth. Because we were all in the same boat, we had nothing to say to one another.

When we finally arrived at Auschwitz, we were ordered to get out of the train. Again the guards screamed: *"Schweine Juden, raus, raus, schnell, schnell!"* "Jewish pigs, out, out, fast, fast!" and they added, "Leave everything behind!" Huge German shepherd dogs with muzzles barked and growled viciously, egged on by their Nazi handlers. We were terribly frightened and did exactly what they told us.

We were told to form two lines, one for women and

children, the other for men and older boys. Families were separated, which was frightening because they depended on one another for comfort and safety. At the front of the line was a man wearing white gloves and a perfectly pressed Nazi SS uniform. He had a strange and scary smile. The inmates knew him as "the Angel of Death." His real name was Dr. Josef Mengele. He had been a doctor before being assigned to Auschwitz. He was evil and a mass murderer. He was only one of many henchmen who worked for Hitler, and they were all evil.

During the twenty-one months that Mengele was at Auschwitz, he did horrible things to the inmates. He was particularly interested in twins, especially identical twins. Because he wanted to study the twins, he had his staff take better care of them than the other inmates. The twins were fed a little more and lived in better housing. Whenever he visited the children, he introduced himself as "Uncle Mengele" and gave them chocolates. All of this made him seem kind, but then he conducted vicious experiments on the twins, most of whom died. When the camp was liberated, only eighty sets of twins had survived out of nearly 3,000 children.

There stood Dr. Mengele before the lines of people coming off the trains. He would point his finger to the right or the left, and each person moved to the appropriate line. None of the arrivals knew it at the time, but a flick of his wrist to the right meant life, while to the left meant death in the gas chambers.

When I reached the front of the line, he pointed to the right for Mila and to the left for Rutka, Macia, and me. I did not think about anyone or anything as I quickly assessed the situation. I somehow understood that one line was going to be killed and the other would live. I thought that if they were separating out young adults, they would be the ones who were spared, perhaps to be used for labor.

In a single moment, I dashed from my line to the line that Mila was on. It did not occur to me that I was leaving my two younger sisters alone on the line leading to the gas chamber. It also did not occur to me that I was burdening Mila with having to keep a child alive in this terrible place and therefore putting her in greater danger. All I knew was that I wanted to live. I did not want to die. Approximately 9,000 people arrived in Auschwitz that day from Sosnowiec. About 90 percent of them died in the gas chamber that day. In all, 30,000 people were brought over a few days as the Nazis made Sosnowiec and the surrounding area *Judenrein*.

As I stood next to Mila, a soldier noticed me. He started yelling and screamed what was a child doing on this line? He began to beat me over the head with the butt of his gun, screaming at me in German. Then he stopped, because he could no longer send me back to the other line, which already had disappeared, and we never saw those people again. I guess he figured that I would die one way or another.

Just then I realized that I had left my two baby sisters on the line to die all alone. Now it was too late to do anything about it. My instant decision was final, and I stayed with Mila.

We were ushered forward in a wave of people through the infamous front gate that lied with its words wrought out of iron, *Arbeit Macht Frei*, which meant "Work Makes You Free." Soon we would learn that neither one's amount of work, how fast one worked, nor how well one worked made anyone free.

Mila and I moved along with the group. We marched for about two miles to the adjacent Birkenau camp. Then we were sent to the showers. We were afraid that we were really being sent to the gas chambers, because we had heard that the gas chambers had fake showerheads and soap to make them look like real showers. The Nazis told the people on the line to the left, the one to the gas chambers, that they were going to the showers, their clothing would be cleaned of lice, and then they would be fed. The Nazis lied so that the people would go quietly and not cause trouble.

Stationed at the real showers were slave workers who took our clothes and whatever possessions we might still have had. They shaved off our hair and gave us a tin bowl, tattered clothes, and wooden clogs. The dress I received reached to the floor, because there was no children's clothing (all children with the exception of twins were sent directly to the gas chambers). The workers tattooed our arms with a number. Now we all looked alike. They had stolen our hair, our clothes, and even our names. We had lost our identities.

From this time forward, we would be referred to only by our numbers. Even today, my left forearm bears a blue tattoo: the number 52643 with a triangle under it. The triangle marked me as a Jew.

Only the inmates at Auschwitz, not at other camps, were given tattoos. The tattoos were initially applied with a special metal stamp with interchangeable numbers. When this became unwieldy, the Nazis used a needle to mark the number on the arm of the prisoner. No one was ever given anesthetic to numb the pain of this procedure. My number, which will always be with me, is a constant reminder of what the Jews suffered at the hands of the Nazis.

People without names or possessions have no sense of self and are less likely to rebel or cause trouble. This worked well at Auschwitz and other concentration camps, where prisoners' serial numbers were merely sewn onto their prison uniforms.

All the women were then taken to a barrack, each of which had a number. The barracks were long wooden buildings that were primitive inside. Birkenau was built as a Polish army base situated on a marsh. Each barrack was fitted with many bunk beds, three tiers high. Ten people shared each bed, which was just a plank of wood, and there was only one thin blanket per bunk. Prisoners slept head to foot. There were only sixteen inches of space allotted to each person. If one person wanted to turn over, everyone had to turn over.

There was an eerie silence inside the barrack, because the women did not speak. There was a woman in charge of each barrack called a *blockaelteste*. The inmates referred to them as *kapo*s. We were responsible for making our plank beds each morning, with hospital corners. If the bed was not made perfectly, the *kapo* would beat whoever was responsible. We quickly learned not to scream or cry, because it only increased our punishment.

This would be our new home. Mila and I found a bunk and lay down next to each other. Before I knew it, the *kapo* was yelling, telling us to get outside and line up. This assembly was called the *appell*. We had to line up in rows and wait to be counted.

Even the sick had to find their places in line. Often, ill

52

inmates were held upright by a person on each side, trying hard not to draw attention to themselves. Those who had died during the night were placed in a pile at the side.

Sometimes we stood at these outdoor roll calls for hours. They always began in the middle of the night. It did not matter if it was freezing cold, snowing, or raining. We stood at attention, waiting, waiting to be counted. We did not have winter clothes, raincoats, or boots. We had only our rags and wooden clogs. We did not even have underwear or socks.

These harsh conditions were why so many inmates got sick. Weather was one of our enemies. Another was starvation. Each day we received a bowl of green water for breakfast, and watery soup and a slice of bread, made mostly from sawdust, later in the day. These rations amounted to approximately 300 calories per day.

Each inmate had a bowl that she kept with her all the time. No bowl, no food! So we guarded our bowls. We never left them unattended, because they could be stolen. We even slept at night with the bowls under our heads. There were not enough calories in the food to keep us healthy, and we rapidly lost weight. I looked like a child of seven, even though by now I was twelve years old.

The only comfort I had was that I was near Mila. For most of the time we lived in Auschwitz, we neither showered nor washed our clothes. We had lice and infected sores from scratching the bites. Many of us got typhus from the lice. This disease causes a high fever, and the patient may become unconscious. Many inmates died from typhus. Both Mila and I contracted this disease. I actually caught it twice.

Even though it was my greatest wish to be with Mila, we did not talk to each other. We did not talk about our past or our hopes for the future as sisters might. We did not discuss our family members, whom we believed were all dead. In fact, I did not remember that I had even had a home or a past life. We just existed side by side. We were exhausted and malnourished. Just surviving was all we could manage to do. We slept next to each other every night, but the joy we once felt at being together was gone, stolen from us in the prime of our lives.

CHAPTER 8
Work in the Camp

All the inmates had to work daily. I wouldn't really call it work, because usually when you work you create something. Work at Auschwitz was really like torture. We carried rocks from one place to another and then back again! Have you ever seen a rock as big as a baby? I did. In fact, I carried it!

Beatings during work were routine. And the purpose of this "work" was to wear people down. Because we were already starving, the loss of calories used in work caused us to become weaker and sicker, often causing death.

Moving rocks was not the only work I did. Our section of the camp held the sewing barrack. Jobs in this barrack were considered special. These jobs were a little easier, because they were indoors. Luckily, I was sent there to work. The strange part is that I could not sew; I had never learned. My job was to deliver clothing to those who could sew. The seamstresses repaired the inmates' clothing, which was changed every few months. Being inside, away from the harsh weather, made this a better job. Unfortunately, I only had this job for two weeks.

Some people today mistake this sewing barrack for the one called "Canada." Canada was where all the goods the Jews brought with them to Auschwitz were collected. These victims were generally those who had not been living in ghettos, but had been taken directly from their homes to the camps. These Jews were told to bring essentials for "relocation," which implied that they were being given a new home. In reality they were to be killed and would not need any possessions, so everything they brought with them was sent to "Canada."

Here their clothing and valuables were prepared to be distributed to German citizens. Sometimes laborers sorting the clothes would find hidden food in them. This was an unexpected benefit, like a gift. It gave those workers a bit more food with which to survive. If food was found, the inmate would hide it and later take it to the barrack. Once again smuggling was important; it often made the difference for survival.

Canada was a large building, given that nickname because the inmates believed that the real Canada was a land of plenty. In this building there was plenty of everything. Clothing, silverware, musical instruments, jewelry, suitcases, food—especially canned goods—shoes, toothbrushes, photos, or anything that people might carry with them in a suitcase for a move to a new place. There were also religious objects, such as Chanukah menorahs, spice boxes, and covers for challah, the Sabbath bread. Most religious items were not sent to Germany. But, if those items were made of silver, they were sent back to Germany and used to pay for the German war effort.

Toward the end of the war, I was sent to Brzezinka, an area of Birkenau, which was a nearby subcamp of Auschwitz. Birkenau had four gas chambers, from which we were separated by an electrified fence. There I sorted clothing to be sent to Germany. The clothing and other items we handled had come directly from the bodies of those to be killed. Sometimes we found food in the clothing. A man on the other side of the fence begged for food. At great risk to my own life, I gave him some.

Years later in America, a man who introduced himself to me as Mr. Engel revealed he was that man on the other side of the fence. He had also survived the war. I was not supposed to go near the fence, and the smallest transgression brought grave consequences. But I did it without thinking.

Our time in the camp dragged slowly by. One day Mila got sick, and she was sent to the Revier, which is what they called the sick bay. The people sent there did not receive any special care. Their clothes were taken away; they were given a place to lie down and a thin blanket to cover them. Everything was filthy, especially the blankets, which were passed from one sick inmate to another. There was no medicine available, and the conditions were horrible. In a way, this almost ensured that people would become even sicker.

I had an important and scary decision to make. Usually when someone was sent to the Revier, they died there or were sent to the gas chambers because they could no longer work. I did not want Mila to go to the Revier alone, so I went with her, even though I was not sick. This meant that there was a strong chance that I too would become sick.

In the Revier, we met a young Jewish woman, about twenty-three years old, named Bozenka. She had been in nursing school in Prague, Czechoslovakia, before the war. She was one of three people who survived in her transport of a thousand people. Now she was in charge of the sick barrack at Birkenau, where ill Jewish inmates were housed. She took care of distributing food to the patients. There could have been as many as 200 sick people in this barrack at any one time. Bozenka took a liking to me, maybe because I looked like a small child. I was unaware at first that she even noticed me. She would end up saving my life more than once.

One day, Bozenka called me down from the third-tier bunk that Mila and I shared. She told me that Dr. Mengele was coming to liquidate the Revier, which happened often. Mila had become sicker and sicker, and it was certain that she would be sent to the gas chamber. I considered going with Mila, even if I had to die with her. Bozenka's helpers told her to send me with Mila, even though I was not sick. Bozenka did not send me. Maybe she just wanted to be sure that this particular child survived, regardless of the consequences to herself.

Again I had to make my own decision. I knew from experience that they would take Mila, my beautiful, kind sister, and throw her limp body onto a cart to the gas chamber. It was horrible to think that Mila would be treated like a carcass. I decided not to go with Mila. There was something inside of me that would not give up and give the Nazis another victory. It was the last time I saw my beloved Mila.

Bozenka decided to take care of me from then on. She decided I would be safer if I went to the Gentile barrack, and so she hid me there. In general, barracks were often divided by specific groups. Jews were not housed with Gentiles. The twins whom Mengele used for experiments had their own barrack; men and women had separate camps separated by electrified barbed-wire fences. Gypsies, political prisoners, Jehovah's Witnesses, priests, nuns, prisoners of war, and a variety of other groups were kept separate from the Jewish inmates.

Bozenka believed that it would be easier to keep me safe

from the gas chamber in the Gentile barrack. In fact, it wasn't easy to protect anyone. One day, Mengele came through the Gentile barrack, searching for hidden Jews. He did not see me, because I was hiding under the blanket of two Christian ladies. Again it was lucky that I was so small!

I returned from the Gentile barrack to the Revier after it had been emptied. Soon I came down with my first bout of typhus. I was very sick, and the disease dragged on for weeks. One day, I thought I must be seeing things when a group of Jewish men entered our barrack. Except for the Gestapo, I had not seen any men in Auschwitz since we had arrived. And yet here they were. They were electricians and had come to do some repairs.

Among the men was a fifteen-year-old boy named Yossie. He began to sing. I could not believe my ears — not only was there suddenly a song in the Revier, but the boy was singing "Kol Nidre," the opening prayer of Yom Kippur, the holiest of our holidays.

A rush of memories came upon me, and I saw my family, especially my mother, in a white embroidered apron she wore on Shabbat to light candles. I could almost smell the golden chicken soup and see the roast chicken and a special kugel (pudding) on the Shabbat table. I saw my bed with clean linens and a soft pillow in a warm house with candles glowing throughout. Mother was hovering over me, giving me a feeling of peacefulness.

Something stirred in me, something that I had long ago suppressed—hope. Hope that Yossie would survive; hope that he would be the witness to Auschwitz, the sole survivor to tell the world; and hope for Jewish continuity. I counted the days until the men would return. I hung on to the thought that I would once again hear Yossie sing, as he was my glimmer of life. But when the men returned, Yossie did not. He had been selected for the gas chamber.

I was so weak, I could barely stand the next time Dr. Mengele strode into the barracks to decide who was going to the gas chamber. Those people he selected had their numbers written on a list and were to be taken by truck to the gas chamber.

Bozenka quickly came to the side of my cot. She urged me

to get up, but I could not move. She whispered urgently that I must save myself, that I must get up and talk to Mengele! The idea sounded absurd. No one spoke to Dr. Mengele and certainly not to beg for one's life. He held supreme control in the camp in matters of life and death. People lived or died according to his whims.

Bozenka got me off the cot to a standing position and propelled me toward where Dr. Mengele stood, smiling. I wore rags. I now stood in front of him and began to speak with great difficulty. "Please take my number off the list." He said in a reassuring tone, "Don't worry, little one. You will be fine."

He began to turn away from me, when a deafening air-raid siren sounded. I looked at Mengele's face and saw that it had turned white! The powerful Dr. Mengele was afraid of an air-raid siren that had been set off by Allied planes taking aerial photos of the Auschwitz complex. They were taking photos of the factories at Buna in hopes of later dropping bombs to disrupt the delivery of war equipment.

Once again Bozenka pushed me forward to ask Mengele

to remove my number from the list of those going to the gas chambers. That air-raid siren was my savior. Mengele was so disoriented and scared that he said yes. I could not believe my ears. Still, I had to ask one more thing. I knew that the assistant whose job it was to write down the numbers of those who were going to die would neither listen to, nor believe, me if I asked him to remove my number from his list.

As bravely as I could, I stepped forward and got Dr. Mengele's attention. "Please tell them to remove my number from the list. They will not do it without orders from you."

He waved backward to his assistant. "Take her number off." And then as quickly as possible he ran from the Revier to his waiting car, which whisked him to safety. At that moment, the assistant turned to Bozenka and said, "I did not hear him, what did he say?" Bozenka told the assistant that several of the numbers were to be removed according to Dr. Mengele's orders.

It worked! Actually, not at first. The assistant stated that no one ever gets off the list. Bozenka had to do a lot of fast talking to get the assistant to comply with her request. Eventually, with Bozenka's help, the man removed five numbers from his list. Bozenka saved five people from death that day. She was a brave person. The assistant easily could have gotten angry and had her shot, or sent her to the gas chamber for defying him. It was a good thing the assistant was in just as big a hurry as Mengele to get to a safe place!

CHAPTER 9
The Death March

My time in the Revier was not over. I contracted a second bout of typhus and was severely ill again. I awoke one day to find myself in a bunk. Having just awakened from a coma, I was extremely weak and confused. The war was nearing its end. The Americans were advancing from the west, and the Russians were approaching even closer from the east.

The Nazis decided to get rid of the evidence of their horrific crimes against the Jewish people and others. They made the decision to empty the camps before the Russians arrived. But what should they do with the remaining inmates? The Germans did not have many options. The gas chambers were no longer operational nor were the crematoria, where they burned the bodies. To destroy evidence of their mass murders, the Germans had blown them up. They decided to remove the survivors and take them elsewhere. Cruelly, they would make the inmates walk to the next destination.

It was a bitter-cold winter, the temperature sometimes reaching forty degrees below zero, with snow on the ground. The inmates had only their ragged clothing and clogs, which were not appropriate for winter weather. In my weak state, I could not walk far, but once again Bozenka came to my rescue. She found a little cart and was able to pull me in the cart until disaster befell us. The cart fell apart. She quickly found a chair and put me on it. Then she turned the chair around and pulled it behind her. This worked for a little while, but it too fell apart.

At this point I began to walk, but not quickly enough to keep pace with the others. When Bozenka saw the soldiers point a gun at me, she did the only thing left for her to do — she carried me! Assisting me did not stop Bozenka from helping others. Whenever I was walking on my own, she walked with one inmate in front of her and one behind her. She kept these two people upright and moving along, always with an eye on me. It was important to keep moving, because anyone who stopped or fell was usually shot on the spot.

The Nazis may have figured that between those who

would die from exposure and those they shot on the road, there would be few inmates left when they reached their destination. In fact, the death march from Auschwitz, which departed on January 18, 1945, began with 66,000 inmates. They abandoned Auschwitz just nine days before the Soviet Red Army liberated the camp on January 27. The Soviets found only 7,000 sick prisoners in the camp, who had been left to die of starvation. Later it was discovered that approximately 1.1 million Jews died at Auschwitz, as well as tens of thousands of other people.

The march continued nearly thirty-five miles to the town of Wodzislaw Slaski, which was, at that time, part of Germany. Along the way, more than 15,000 perished. We usually just dropped to the ground at night wherever we were. It could be an open field, a road, or a forested area. I remember that we once stayed overnight in a barn.

When we reached Wodzislaw Slaski, the inmates were put in open freight cars and transported to other camps. Again it was bitter cold, and we had no way to hide from the fierce wind and snow. This was actually a small blessing. We were able to eat a little of the snow just by letting the flakes fall into our mouths. The snow helped wet our parched throats and lips, because the guards had not given us any water along the way.

It was difficult to calculate just how long we walked and then rode on the train. Eventually we arrived at the Ravensbrück concentration camp, located in northern Germany, about fifty miles north of Berlin. There was no room in the camp barracks for us, so we just sat on the ground in the snow. There was one tent, which created shelter for some.

When it was time to leave Ravensbrück, the guards did not want to let me go with the group I had come in with. This meant I would be separated from Bozenka. She was not about to let that happen. She organized a group of women to surround me and hide me within their circle, away from the eyes of the guards. The women shuffled off as a group to the train with me in the middle and successfully got me on the train to the Neustadt-Glewe subcamp.

Neustadt-Glewe was also in Germany. The inmates of Ravensbrück and Auschwitz were brought here so the

Germans did not have to free them, because it was in their own territory. It was an easy way to consign more Jews to death. There were Poles kept here as well. This work camp provided labor for a company that produced airplanes. Those who did not work received the worst rations, so many died of starvation.

Once again, Bozenka came to my rescue. She shared her rations with me. The camp was liberated on May 2, 1945, by the Soviet Red Army. We were finally free. Soon after our liberation, Bozenka found a cow so she could provide milk for me. She cared for me as she would have for her own child.

CHAPTER 10
The Long Way Home

After our liberation I did not know what to do. I was frightened. I felt alone in the world. The only person left in my life was Bozenka. She kindly offered to take me home to her remote village of Tvrdosin in Czechoslovakia, now the Slovak Republic. She had already done so much for me, and she wanted to return home.

I could not go home to Jaworzno, certainly not alone, because it was too dangerous. The family home no longer belonged to me. And I did not expect to find any members of my immediate family there. I believed that they had all died at the hands of the Nazis. Indeed, I believed that all eleven sets of aunts, uncles, and their children on my mother's side had been murdered. I was now fourteen years old, had no family, and was weary of being alone.

So off with Bozenka I went. This time I walked under my own power. When we arrived at her home, she learned that her parents and brother had been hiding in Czechoslovakia and had survived. They also owned a hotel with a large courtyard.

Bozenka's family was able to enroll me in school, even though I could neither read nor speak Slovakian. I quickly picked up the language, and the principal told Bozenka that I was the best student in the school.

I must admit that in my child's mind I was a little afraid of Bozenka, this stranger in my life who was a guardian angel to me. I believed that I was not a good person, because I had left my two baby sisters to die alone and then didn't go with Mila to the gas chamber. I thought that as soon as Bozenka realized that I was "no good," she would hate me, even leave me. I did not realize that she did not save me because of who I was, but rather because of who *she* was.

Although Bozenka was Jewish, she was not observant, so all the elements of faith that I longed for—Shabbat, holidays, kosher food—were not to be had. On the other hand, clothing, food, safety, and a home were critical to my survival. Bozenka provided all my everyday needs. She was a saintly woman.

It is written in the Torah, the scroll of Jewish law, that if a person saves even one life, it is as if they have saved the entire world. This means that if you save a person's life, and that person goes on to have children, and those children have children, and so on, you are responsible for saving all of them. If you had not saved the first person, then the others would not exist. And who knows what wonderful things they might achieve in their lifetimes, such as a cure for cancer or the end to hunger.

Because of Bozenka, I survived to have children, and they had children, and someday my grandchildren will have children. Generations of my family far into the future will remember the strength and kindness of Bozenka, because we will remember the past, and others will pass it on.

One day, there was a knock at the door of Bozenka's home. There stood a man who said he knew me, and I recognized him. It was my cousin Asher, from Jaworzno. Asher's mother and my mother were sisters. He was excited and happy to find me. He had been looking for cousins on his father's side of the family in a Polish border town called Teschen, and he had met someone who knew my name and knew where I was. He managed to cross the border to Czechoslovakia to come see me. Then he told me something that sounded impossible — that he had seen my oldest brother, Mendek, just the week before.

I calmly answered that he must be mistaken. I was sure that my brother hadn't survived the camps he had been sent to. Asher smiled again and firmly said, "Your brother Mendek is alive. I saw him about one week ago."

I was astonished. Mendek had survived? I couldn't believe it. How strange it felt that someone in my immediate family had survived besides me. Asher said that I should go with him to see my brother.

Now I had to say good-bye to Bozenka. But this was not easy. She had been my guardian for the last year and a half. She had carried me when she could have left me at the side of the road, where I would have died. She cared for me like a mother cares for a child, but my life had to be with my brother Mendek now. Bozenka even suggested that my cousin let me remain with her and that she would always take care of me. Asher of course had to decline her offer. Bozenka understood and sent me on my way with my cousin to reconnect with my brother and pick up the pieces of my former life.

When Asher and I finally arrived in Germany, I was anxious to see Mendek, whom I had not seen in four years. When we met, I almost did not recognize him. He was tall and thin, but it was definitely Mendek. I was never so glad to see anyone. Mendek did not want to talk about the painful things he had endured, so we left it at being happy to be together.

Mendek and I were in Weiden, Germany, where we stayed with cousins on Mother's side of the family. We knew that there were some family members who lived in America, but we did not have any idea of how to contact them. Suddenly, we were contacted by our cousin Simon from Brooklyn, New York.

Cousin Simon had lived in Vienna, Austria, with his family. As he grew up, he became a soccer star on the major-league Jewish soccer team and was famous in Vienna. When the Nazis first started gaining power in Germany, they often beat up Jews on the street. This happened not only in Germany, but also Austria, where anti-Semitism became rampant. Simon did not like his country's Nazi sympathizers, so after dark he would go out onto the streets of Vienna and beat up anyone who had hurt Jews that day. He built a reputation as a troublemaker, and the Nazis began to look for him. He decided it was time to get out of Europe and left for America in 1938.

Simon found an apartment in the Boro Park section of Brooklyn, New York. Soon after, Simon successfully brought his parents, brother, and sister-in-law to the United States directly out of a concentration camp. They arrived in New York City one day before the attack on Pearl Harbor, which occurred December 7, 1941. This was nearly impossible to do. They moved into the one-bedroom apartment with him. Eventually he got married and had children. After the war was over, he began to look for survivors from our family. We made contact with him, and in 1946 we were on our way to New York City on the ship named the *Marine Perch*, which departed from Hamburg, Germany.

The trip was uneventful except for one thing: I became very nauseous on the ship. This was really sad because they had so much food, as much as you wanted, and I could not eat.

They offered me bananas, oranges, and ice cream, which were real luxuries, and something I had never eaten or even seen before: peanut butter. I still don't eat peanut butter because it makes me nauseous to even think about it!

When the ship docked in New York Harbor, I was the last passenger to be transferred to the immigration facility at Ellis Island. I was escorted directly to a ward of Ellis Island's hospital. There was only a skeleton crew on duty. It was a holiday, and most of the staff had the day off. That meant that they did not have translators available. I did not speak English, and my other languages did not help much with communication. The immigration officials did not want to let me enter the country. They believed that I had tuberculosis, a contagious lung disease.

Once again I felt like a prisoner, because the officials had to confine me in the hospital on the island until they could determine what I had and if it was contagious. I was confused, scared, and lonely. Finally a diagnosis was made. Hooray, it was not tuberculosis! They released me, and I was on my way to living in America.

I was now fifteen years old and still had not been to school for any length of time. School administrators decided to put me in high school, where I began learning English during the first year.

It was a difficult year even though everyone was nice to me. In my mind, I thought I was not learning enough, especially not English. I believed that if I wrote down every English word I learned and looked it up in a German dictionary, I would understand more of the language. One teacher helped me a lot, and I began to realize that I knew more than I gave myself credit for. I learned to read and write and caught up with all the usual school subjects. But I also had to learn about the culture of the United States, which was so different from what I had experienced up to that time.

During the summer, I studied on my own and then took the Regents (standardized state tests) in Hebrew and German to fulfill the high school's foreign-language requirement. I passed with high marks. The teacher who taught German was so excited about my abilities that she took me to meet the principal and a group of teachers, who interviewed me.

I wanted to impress them about how handy Mendek was, so I told them that he was "handicapped," mistakenly thinking that this word meant he was highly skilled. Everyone had a good laugh over that one!

I graduated with honors from high school in just three years. I even took commercial courses, such as typing and stenography, so that I would be able to get a job in business to help support myself. I did get a job and attended Brooklyn College at night. I graduated from college magna cum laude, an honor that attested to my abilities to pass every class with the highest grades.

Later on I attended Adelphi College to earn a Master of Science in Education degree. I was able to take most of my courses in Manhattan, where Adelphi had a campus. However, I also had to take courses at the main campus in Long Island in order to finish the degree. This meant that I had to travel by train and then by cab to get to my classes. When you want to succeed at something, you do whatever you have to do. I really wanted to succeed.

How ironic was it that I became an ESL (English as a

Second Language) teacher? Well, that's what happened! I loved teaching and continued to do so until I retired.

My future husband, Ephraim, came from Tarnobrzeg, Poland, and then was sent to Siberia in the Soviet Union, where he stayed with his parents and sister throughout World War II. As difficult as Siberia was, they were fortunate in that they were not sent to ghettos, slave-labor camps, or concentration camps where they might have been killed. When they immigrated to the United States after the war, they moved to the Lower East Side of New York.

I met Ephraim through a religious Jewish organization that decided to have a summer picnic in Spring Valley, New York, for young singles. We met there and talked to each other, but he did not ask me out right away. He waited until after the Jewish New Year, Rosh Hashanah, which is a pious time of year. He wanted my family to recognize that he was a serious young man. When he did ask me out, I quickly said yes, and we began dating.

We got married in March 1953 and decided to live in

Brooklyn, about two blocks away from my cousin's home. We still live in the same area today. Ephraim got a job working with Mendek and Simon. I became a mother. One daughter became a lawyer, and the other a teacher. One daughter had two children, both boys, making me a grandma, or as we say in Yiddish, a *babbi*, and my husband a *zaidy*!

Mendek also went to high school in Brooklyn after the war, but he attended at night, because he had to work during the day. He went into the jewelry business with our cousin Simon, who was a tool and die maker. Simon and Mendek invented machines for the jewelry business. The machines were used to set stones such as diamonds and emeralds, a process that had always been done by hand. The machines were much faster.

They also created a clasp for bracelets that is still used by the jewelry industry today. These inventions were patented. Simon and Mendek were like efficiency experts. When they saw a problem, they would find a solution, creating new machines.

Mendek was drafted into the United States Army during

the Korean War. I was so upset that they would send him to war, after all he had been through, that I wrote a letter to his draft board describing what had happened to him since he was a teenager. The army was less than sympathetic. They said that if he could survive all that he had been through, then he was just what the army needed. They also said that he should be grateful to the United States for having liberated him from the camps and therefore should want to serve his new country. So off to Korea he went, to participate in yet another war. Luckily for our family and for him, Mendek returned safely to us.

Mendek met his future wife, Edith, in Israel. They married and then lived in New York City. Together they raised two girls, Ruth and Myra. Both girls went to college in California and decided to settle there. After Myra grew up, she decided to run a special farm and business that sold prewashed bagged lettuce and other organic vegetables. It was a new concept, and it gradually became successful, mainly because Mendek, in his usual fashion, invented the machines needed to help clean and bag the vegetables for sale. Today they sell their products all over the United States and are one of these types of products' largest producers. Mendek also now lives in California.

CHAPTER II
Speaking Out

As an adult, I never spoke about my experiences from the war. I just kept quiet about those years and the horrors I had survived. I also never laughed or cried.

The first thing to change was the laughing. I went on a family trip to Israel. I had never been there before, even though we had some cousins living there. I loved being in Israel, seeing the independent nation that my brethren had created. I was happy to see that they had turned this barren piece of land into a self-sufficient, thriving, green country. It was special to visit the many places in Israel that are a part of our history such as the Kotel, the Western Wall of our holy temple, which is more than two thousand years old.

I was so excited to be in our free Jewish homeland that I just started to laugh. My daughter said, "Mom, do you know that you are laughing? I never see you laugh!" I hadn't realized it. After that day, many other things made me laugh. I've learned that the world is more exciting and wondrous since the war ended than I ever imagined. For example, just hearing a certain type of opera singer—a coloratura soprano—was amazing to me. Now I laugh a lot!

The next thing to change was telling my life story, including the good times and the bad. This was hard to do. I had just retired from teaching at an elementary school and was looking for something different and meaningful to do, for others as well as for me. I had read in the paper that the new Museum of Jewish Heritage: A Living Memorial to the Holocaust in Battery Park, New York, was willing to train people to become docents (museum guides and educators).

This meant I would have to learn all about the museum's core displays and how to explain them to visitors. I needed to learn how to speak to children of different ages as well as adults. I decided to give it a try. I discovered that I liked being at the museum and interacting with the visitors. However, I still had never told anyone my own story, which was too painful.

One of the docents with whom I had become friendly

felt that it was time for me to share my story. Bertha kept encouraging me, so one day I took a relaxation medicine and told my story for the first time.

The audience was comprised of about one hundred docents in training. I got up in front of them and gradually spoke about my personal story, but did not talk about the members of my family. I thought I was doing terribly and that the museum would never use me again as a speaker. The audience, however, listened intently.

When I was done, they applauded, and that was the beginning of the most challenging job I have ever known. But, I liked it! Not long after that, I was sent to a high school, where for the first time I decided to talk about my siblings. The students' response was so strong that from that time on I began to speak about my siblings all the time.

Since then I have spoken to thousands of museum visitors and visited hundreds of schools. I have shared the wonderful beginning to my life; my misfortunes during the war, including showing students my tattooed concentration-camp number; and my life after the war. I am gratified by the responses I have received, from young children to college students to people my own age, especially to the concept that they now must carry on the story and never allow these evils to occur again.

As for the third thing I hadn't done since the war — crying — that is still a missing piece of my life. When we were young during the war, we learned quickly that crying did not get you anything. No one had sympathy for a crying child, especially when the adults in our life could not give children the things they were crying about. During the war, parents, grandparents, older siblings, and extended family members could not even produce so much as a lollipop to make a child happy. To this day I do not cry, but I remember and share my story.

CHAPTER 12
Your Responsibility

This is the end of my story, but not the end of the story of the Holocaust. Today there are many people who say that the Holocaust did not happen. They believe that the Jews just want the rest of the world to feel sorry for them and for Israel. But the Holocaust did happen. I remember exactly what took place. I have the number on my arm that places me in Auschwitz during those terrible years. I remember smuggling food into the ghetto to try to save my family from starvation. And I remember how frightened I was as a nine-year-old who had no choice but to put her life on the line to save others. Holocaust deniers can deny whatever they want, but I was there, and except for Mendek, my whole family was wiped out.

Stories have a moral or lesson. It is your job to learn the story of the Holocaust and tell it to others. Remember what took place and help others see that the world must not allow it to happen again. We must be humane in our dealings with others. To be kind and caring toward one another is vital. Each of us must look for ways to protect others who are at risk. To save one life is as if you have saved the whole world. That must be our goal.

Acknowledgments

I am grateful to Carol Bierman for her unfailing confidence in me, for her perseverance in getting this book written and published. Without her, this book would not have come to fruition. Thank you to my husband, Ephraim, for his sage advice and for always being there for me with a helping hand. Thank you to my children for giving me their wholehearted support. Thank you to my grandchildren, who give meaning to my life.

—*B.B.*

Many thanks to my husband, Michael, and to all my children and grandchildren, who believed in my efforts to record this story. Thanks also to my editor, Roy Wandelmaier, for his patience and direction and for giving us a chance to tell this important story. Thanks to Lola Kaufman for sharing and directing me to a fabulous publisher.

—*C.B.*